METHODIST RECORDS
FOR FAMILY HISTORIANS

Richard Ratcliffe

THE FAMILY HISTORY PARTNERSHIP

Published by
The Family History Partnership
57 Bury New Road, Ramsbottom
Bury, Lancashire BL0 0BZ

www.thefamilyhistorypartnership.com

First edition published 2014

ISBN: 978 1 906280 44 4

Printed and bound by
Berforts Information Press
Southfield Road, Eynsham
Oxford OX29 4JB

Contents

1. INTRODUCTION

The Methodist movement was founded at Oxford University in November 1729 by a small group of students which included John Wesley, Fellow of Lincoln College and son of the Rev. Samuel Wesley of Epworth in Lincolnshire and his wife Susannah [nee Annesley]. Other members of this group included John's younger brother Charles a student at Christ Church College and William Morgan of Christ Church College, Robert Kirkham of Merton College and Messrs Ingham of Queen's College, Broughton of Exeter College and Clayton of Brazenose College. Later they were joined by George Whitfield who was to encourage John Wesley to become an open air preacher.

This small group became known as the "Bible Moths" or "Methodists" because of their methodical and austere way of life, their daily bible study and prayer meetings which were in sharp contrast to the way of life of other students.

After graduating in Divinity and Classics in 1724 and qualifying for his M.A. in 1725, John became a deacon of the Church of England in 1726, was elected Fellow of Lincoln College in 1727 qualifying him to become a teacher and lecturer, a post which he took up in 1729. In 1735 he went as a missionary and chaplain to Georgia in America. After a disastrous two years in Georgia, John returned to England in a very depressed state in February 1738. On May 24th, 1738, John attended a meeting of the Moravian Society [a German Protestant group], in Aldersgate Street, London where *"At about a quarter to nine, I felt my heart strangely warmed. I felt I did trust in Christ, Christ alone for salvation, and an assurance was given me, that he had taken away my sins, even mine, and saved me from the law of sin and death."*

From that moment onwards he set out to evangelise the Church of England, reform the Poor Law, the Penal Code, improve conditions in the prisons and stop the exploitation of labour in the factories and mines.

2. THE METHODIST MOVEMENT 1739-1791

Between 1739 and his death in 1791, Wesley travelled the length and breadth of the British Isles and was especially effective as a preacher in London, Cornwall, Yorkshire and the industrial centres of Bristol, Manchester, Newcastle on Tyne and Birmingham. He is said to have travelled 250,000 miles on horseback and preached 40,000 sermons in his 52 year ministry. By the time of his death on March 2nd, 1791 at the age of 88, the Methodist Movement had 70,000 members and half a million adherents.

Initially John Wesley was supported and encouraged by George Whitfield, but by 1741 the two men and their followers had fallen out over their differing interpretations of the Gospel. Whitfield supported the Calvinist Doctrine of Predestination, while Wesley favoured the Arminian Doctrine of Justification by Faith. The two men remained on cordial terms right up to Whitfield's death in 1770. Wesley encouraged his followers to build preaching houses or chapels for worship and prayer meetings; Whitfield's followers built tabernacles in which they held their preaching services.

Whitfield received much public and financial support from Selina, Countess of Huntingdon to build his tabernacles, especially in Wales, while Wesley relied on his preaching to support the creation of local house meetings to establish viable societies before building preaching houses.

Wesley's *"Journal" [1735-1790]* - his diary of his journeys, meetings and services - is one of the major autobiographies of the 18th Century. It shows that his most effective preaching was in London, Cornwall and Yorkshire, as well as the industrial centres of Bristol, Manchester, Birmingham and Newcastle upon Tyne.

The New Room, Bristol

In 1739, Wesley built the first Methodist Preaching House - the New Room Chapel in the Horsefair in Bristol. This became his headquarters in the South-West of England. He laid the foundation stone on May 12th, 1739 only 5 weeks after preaching his first open air service in Bristol and opened it for public worship on June 3rd. Wesley spent more time in the New Room than any other place during the next 50 years. Here he wrote hundreds of letters and many of his books including his "Book of Physick." Here he trained his travelling preachers and in 1742 started the first Class meetings which were to become the bedrock of Methodism, where people met for Bible reading and prayer as well as pastoral care and assistance. Here in 1771 he commissioned Francis Asbury, to go to America as a missionary where he became the founding father of American Methodism and the first Bishop of the Methodist Episcopal Church in 1784. It was near the New Room that John Wesley's younger brother Charles lived at 4 Charles Street, Bristol from 1749-1771 and where he wrote many of his 6000 hymns.

The Foundery, Moorfields, London

In the same year, 1739, John Wesley bought the remains of the Old Foundery in Moorfields just outside the City of London, refurbished it and made it his London headquarters until he replaced it in 1779 with a new chapel in nearby City Road.

The Foundery was more than a preaching house - it was a free dispensary, a school for pauper children, an almshouse for widows and a lending bank to help people get started in business. One borrower, James Lackington, established a prosperous bookshop known as "The Temple of the Muses" in Finsbury Square in London after borrowing £5 to get established. Later he used his wealth to build a number of Methodist preaching houses including octagonal chapels at Taunton and Budleigh Salterton.

First Conference, 1744

In 1744, Wesley held the first of the Annual Conferences in the Foundery - meetings of his helpers - to confer with them on the doctrines which they should preach, the disciplines which they should exercise and to decide where his preachers should be stationed for the coming year. Following each Annual Conference since 1744, *the Minutes of Conference* have been published and are a valuable source of Methodist history and biography, since they contain details of the circuits and their ministers and obituaries of ministers who have died since the last conference.

In 1783, the Methodist Conference persuaded Wesley to ordain three preachers [Thomas Coke, Richard Vasey and Richard Whatcoat] to go to America where ordained ministers were urgently needed. He did so reluctantly but continued to refuse to ordain any of his preachers in this country so that they could administer the Sacraments. As he was seeking to reform the Anglican Church, he urged his Wesleyan followers to continue to receive Holy Communion in their parish churches.

3. SPLITS, DIVISIONS and UNITY 1791-1932

Within a few years of the death of John Wesley in 1791, the Wesleyan Movement had broken away from the Church of England and had become the Wesleyan Methodist Church. In the course of the next 50 years, several groups broke away from the Wesleyan Church most of whom used the name Methodist.

Methodist New Connexion
The first breakaway group was the **Methodist New Connexion** [MNC]. The MNC came into being on August 9th, 1797 when Alexander Kilham, William Thom, Stephen Eversfield and Alexander Cummin met at the Ebenezer Chapel in Leeds and formally set up the MNC after the refusal of the Wesleyan Methodist Conference to discuss questions of administration which they felt were vital to the expansion of Methodism. These were:

> *"That the times of Sunday services should be determined by those who wished to attend them and not by an anxiety to avoid the usual hours of services in the Anglican Church."*
>
> *"That lay members of Methodism should share in the government of the Church at Circuit and District meetings and at the Annual Conference of Preachers."*

The MNC quickly took root in the North of England and by 1847 its Golden Jubilee year the MNC had 20,000 members in the UK, 30,000 members in Canada, 141 ministers, 334 chapels and 38,000 Sunday School scholars.

In 1866, the President of the MNC Conference, Rev Stanley Hulme, sent a letter to the Wesleyan Conference suggesting the possibility of exploring the question of Methodist Unity. The Wesleyan President, Rev William Arthur responded with these words, *"We have seen days of division and breaking down. God grant that we may now see days of building up."* Hulme's vision of unity was not realised until 1932.

Primitive Methodists
The second group to breakaway from the Wesleyans were the **Primitive Methodists** led by Hugh Bourne who was born at Fordhays Farm, near Stoke on Trent and

William Clowes a relative of Josiah Wedgwood. Bourne and Clowes were two Wesleyan ministers who in 1807 wanted to bring about a religious revival in the Potteries and the mining villages of North Staffordshire. Through their open air Camp Meetings at Mow Cop near Tunstall in Staffordshire, many people were converted but their membership was not recognised by the Wesleyan Conference. The name Primitive Methodist comes from an address by John Wesley to his preachers in Chester in 1790.

> *"Go out into the streets and lanes of the city and bring in the poor, the maimed, the halt and the blind and this is the way the primitive Methodists did."*

The Primitive Methodists, nicked named "The Ranters" because of their singing in the streets, soon spread into Nottingham, Lincolnshire, Liverpool, West Yorkshire, East Anglia and Essex and later into Cornwall and South Wales. In 1849 the PM Conference recorded a membership of 104,762, 519 ministers, 8524 local preachers and 5170 chapels.

Bible Christians

The third group to break away were the **Bible Christians** founded on the borders of Devon and Cornwall in 1815 by William O'Bryan, a Wesleyan local preacher from Cornwall who had been rejected as a candidate for the Wesleyan ministry. Following a Preaching Service at Lake Farm, Shebbear, Devon on October 9th 1815, 22 members were enrolled and the Bible Christian Movement had been born. Known locally in the West Country as Free Willers, Shining Lights and Bryanites, the Bible Christians grew apace and by 1865 when they celebrated their Golden Jubilee in Exeter they reported 750 chapels, 2000 ministers and local preachers, 26,000 members, 40,000 Sunday School scholars and 8,000 Sunday School teachers. By this time they had spread beyond Devon and Cornwall into Dorset and the Isle of Wight. Significantly they had a higher proportion of female local preachers than the other Methodist denominations. At their Annual Conference of 1831 they agreed to evangelise overseas. For the next 30 years a steady stream of Bible Christian emigrants left the West Country for destinations as far afield as China, Bermuda and New Zealand. The largest numbers went to Canada, with many settling on Prince Edward Island and in what is now Ontario. By the 1860s, levels of emigration were affecting the numbers of adherents at home and the policy of encouraging emigration was less aggressively pursued. For further information see http:// genuki.cs.ncl.ac.uk/DEV/Shebbear/ Bible Christians/ and http://freepages.history.rootsweb.ancestry.com/~bible christian/index.htm/

Other Breakaway Groups

Several smaller groups also broke away from the Wesleyans. These included the **Protestant Methodists** [1827], the **Wesleyan Methodist Association** [1836] and the **Wesleyan Reformers** [1849]. These three groups amalgamated in 1857 to form the **United Methodist Free Church** [UMFC] apart from a small group of Wesleyan Reformers who refused to join and instead formed the Wesleyan Reform Union which continues to exist to this day.

At the time of amalgamation the UMFC had a membership of 40,000, 110 ministers and 769 chapels.

In the meantime, the **Wesleyan Methodist Church** had been making many important changes, such as allocating places at the Annual Conference and at District Meetings to laymen, making Wesley's travelling preachers "ministers" after a 4 year probationary period and also giving them authority to administer Holy Communion/the Sacrament of the Lord's Supper. In 1818 the use of the prefix "Reverend" was authorised.

Towards Union

Moves to unite Methodism proceeded very slowly following the first overtures from the Methodist New Connexion to the Wesleyan Conference in 1866.

In 1907, the United Methodist Free Church, the Methodist New Connexion and the Bible Christians agreed to join together to form the **United Methodist Church** [**UMC**].

Finally in 1932, the United Methodist Church, the Primitive Methodist Church and the Wesleyan Methodist Church came together and formed the **Methodist Church** which has become the much slimmer Methodist Church of today.

4. HOW METHODISM IS ORGANISED

Amalgamation of the administration of the different groups of Methodism was comparatively easy as each group followed the lines of administration devised by John Wesley in 1744. Wesley set out clear lines of communication within the Methodist movement.

There is the Annual Conference [or Assembly] which is the principal decision making body. It is composed of the Chairmen of each of the Districts plus elected ministers and laypersons from each District and confirms the stationing of ministers for the coming church year.

Under the Conference are the Districts, covering several counties in some cases and made up of a large number of Circuits who are answerable to a Chairman of the District.

The half-yearly Synods of the Districts implement decisions taken by the Conference, consider reports from National [Connexional] and District committees and discuss responses to go back to the next Conference as well as electing their representatives to go to Conference.

Each District is divided into a number of Circuits. A circuit is a group of chapels overseen by a Superintendent Minister.

The Quarterly meetings of the circuits implement decisions taken by Conference and passed on from the district synods, elect representatives to attend their district synod and discuss circuit matters, some of which may be referred to the district synod or possibly to Conference.

Each Church or Chapel within a Circuit also holds meetings every quarter to receive information passed down from the circuit meetings and district synods and to discuss responses that may be required by the circuit meetings and district synods as well as dealing with chapel matters. These Quarterly meetings are now called Church Council meetings but were formerly called Trustees' meetings.

All these meetings and the many committees which feed into them have produced masses of documents over the past 260 years, many of which can be of interest to family and local historians.

5. METHODIST BAPTISMAL, MARRIAGE and BURIALS RECORDS

Methodist Baptismal Registers

The early Methodists began to build preaching houses in the 1760s and soon children of Methodists began to be baptised in these meeting places. Few Baptismal Registers survive before 1790 and most children of early Methodists continued to be baptised in the Church of England until after 1800 when the practice of Infant Baptism in Methodist Chapels became more common. In 1812, the Wesleyan Methodist Conference urged churches to register baptisms.

Let that ordinance, if possible, be always administered in the public congregation.

Let us administer it, in general, only to the children of our members and those of our regular hearers.

Let a small fee be taken for registering Baptisms where the parents can afford to pay it; let such fees after defraying the expense of the Register Book be given to the poor.

Soon after the introduction of Civil Registration of Births, Marriages and Deaths in July, 1837, the Non- Parochial Registers Act was passed requiring all Methodist Chapels [and other Nonconformist Churches] to deposit their pre 1837 registers with the Registrar-General. 856 volumes of baptisms and burials from all branches of Methodism were deposited together with the Wesleyan Metropolitan Registry 1818-1838 which contains over 50,000 entries of births and baptisms from across England, Wales and further afield. These records have been microfilmed and can be seen at The National Archives [TNA] at Kew in Class RG4.

They are also accessible online on www.bmdregisters.co.uk which is a pay per view website and is linked to a very informative guide to Nonconformist birth, marriage and death registers held by TNA. The early Methodist baptismal registers have also been microfilmed by the Genealogical Society of Utah [GSU] and are included in the International Genealogical Index or Family Search records of the GSU. A full index of these registers is included in William Leary's book *"My Ancestors were Methodists"* [4th edition], Society of Genealogists Enterprises, 2006.

Before depositing these registers, some ministers made a copy of the register entries. These may now be found in the custody of the present Circuit Superintendent Minister or in the nearest County Record Office [CRO].

One such register - Brigg Primitive Methodist Circuit Baptismal Register 1825-1837 can be seen at the Lincolnshire Archives Office. Baptisms were recorded at Belton [in the Isle of Axholme], Kirton in Lindsey, Scotter, East Stockwith, Corringham, as well as Brigg. The place names give an indication of the size of the Circuit.

The Beverley Wesleyan Circuit Baptismal Register 1827-1876 kept in the East Yorkshire Record Office at Beverley opens with these remarks and entries:

Register of Births and of Baptisms with water solemnized in the name of the Father, of the Son and of the Holy Ghost at various places in the Beverley Circuit. Kept at Beverley in the County of York commencing September 9th 1827.

The entries from Number 1 to Number 37 inclusive are copies, the originals of which were forwarded to London to the Registration Commissioners on July 13th 1837 by me J. Stephenson.

1. *Elizabeth daughter of Robert NICHOLSON of South Cave in the Parish of South Cave in the County of York, Wheelwright and of Ann his wife who was the daughter of Matthew and Elizabeth PICKERING was born 28th July 1827 and baptised with water on 9th September 1827 by me Joseph Hutton.*

2. *Henry son of William POST of Beverley in the Parish of Beverley in the County of York, Labourer, and Mercy his wife was born 4th May 1828 and baptised with water on 7th May 1828 by me Joseph Hutton.*

3. *Robert son of Francis NICHOLSON of Beverley in the Parish of Beverley in the County of York, Shoemaker and of Sarah his wife who was the daughter of James and Hannah VARY was born 22nd July 1826 and baptised with water on 18th August 1828 by me Joseph Hutton.*

4. *Samuel son of Francis NICHOLSON of Beverley in the Parish of Beverley in the County of York, Shoemaker and of Sarah his wife who was the daughter of James and Hannah VARY was born 11th August 1828 and baptised with water on 18th August 1828 by me Joseph Hutton.*

5. *Martha daughter of John WILKINSON of Molescroft in the Parish of Hellary in the County of York, Labourer, and Ann his wife was born 21st September 1828 and baptised with water 30th September 1828 by me Joseph Hutton.*

Most entries in this Register are of children whose parents lived in Beverley but other Parishes mentioned include Skidby, Cottingham, Cherry Burton, St Martin's Beverley, Welton, Molescroft, Bishop Burton, Newbald, Middleton on the Wolds, Eske, Riplingham, Hull Bridge, Tickton, Ellerker and one entry for Uttoxeter in Staffordshire.

Since 1837, Methodist Baptismal Registers have been kept by Ministers of the Methodist Circuits. There are 2 kinds of Baptismal Register which may survive;

[a]   The Circuit Baptismal Register which should contain the names of all children and occasionally adults baptised in the circuit. The entries often include dates of birth as well as dates of baptism, and sometimes the mother's maiden surname. Please note that many circuits included chapels in more than one county.

E.g. Bole [Nottinghamshire] Wesleyan Methodist Chapel was opened in the 1860s but closed in 1950s. Its baptisms can be found in Gainsborough [Lincolnshire] Wesleyan Circuit Registers in the Lincolnshire Archives Office as Bole was in the Gainsborough Wesleyan Circuit even though it is in Nottinghamshire. Other Nottinghamshire Chapels in the Gainsborough Wesleyan Circuit included Beckingham, Walkeringham, West Stockwith, Misterton and Gringley on the Hill. Other examples include the Chipping Norton [Oxfordshire] Wesleyan Circuit Registers in the Oxfordshire History Centre which record baptisms in Shipston on Stour [formerly in Worcestershire], Brailes, Ascott and Long Compton in Warwickshire as well as in chapels in North Oxfordshire, while the Banbury Primitive Methodist Circuit Registers includes baptisms in South Warwickshire, North Oxfordshire and West Northampton-shire chapels.

[b]   The local Chapel Baptismal Register begun in 1837/8 may still be in use in the present chapel. Unfortunately many of these early registers have been lost or are now in private hands such as the families of chapel officers or local historians, but a large number thankfully can be located in the local CRO, in the chapel or circuit safe or even at the minister's manse.

Many chapels have been closed since Methodist Union in 1932, especially where earlier there were 2 or even 3 chapels in the same town or village. The baptismal registers from the closed chapels can often be located in the nearest CRO.

It is well worth checking copies of County Directories of the 19th and early 20th Centuries such as Kelly's or White's to find out how many Methodist Chapels existed in a town or village. These Directories can usually be found in CROs and Local Studies Libraries.

For example in *White's Directory of Lincolnshire* [1856] the entry for Grantham states that *"The Wesleyans, the Primitive Methodists, the Independents, the Calvinists and the Wesleyan Reformers have chapels in the town, and the Wesleyan Chapel in Finkin Street, erected in 1840 to replace a small old chapel has 1300 seats, seven vestries, a schoolroom and a chapel-keeper's house."*

If there are no records for some of those chapels in the CRO you should ask the County Archivist to put you in touch with the Archivist of the present Methodist Circuit or with the District Archivist who may be able to help.

Methodist Marriage Registers

The holding of marriages in Methodist chapels was legalised in 1837, but not every chapel was registered. Where a chapel was registered, the local Registrar had to attend and record the marriage in the chapel register which he kept at the Register Office. Every quarter, the Registrar would forward a copy to his Superintendent Registrar who in turn would forward a copy to the Registrar General to be indexed at Somerset House. The chapel itself did not keep an official marriage register, but some ministers kept "unofficial" registers and these can sometimes be found in CROs if they survive or even among family papers of a former minister.

The Marriage Act of 1898 meant that the attendance of Registrars at marriages in Methodist chapels was not always required as previously. A number of Methodist ministers were now legally appointed to conduct and register marriages in specified chapels. Where a chapel was not registered, the Registrar still had to attend, and this still applies today.

Methodist marriage registers which are duplicates of civil registers after 1837 may be found in 2 places. Where a chapel has been closed but was previously registered for marriages, the register should be located in the CRO. Where the chapel is still in use and registered, the marriage register is kept by the minister in the chapel or circuit safe. A fee may be chargeable for a search. Please note that these registers are not usually indexed.

Methodist Burial Registers

The Wesleyan Methodist Conference of 1803 ordered that a Register of Deaths of members of each Methodist Society should be kept in every circuit. This order does not appear to have been very strictly observed judging by the small number of Burial/Death Registers listed in the list of registers surrendered to the Registrar General in 1837. It may have been ignored because few chapels had any adjoining land that could be used as a burial ground, except perhaps in Liverpool, Lancashire and the West Riding of Yorkshire. Where burial grounds are still open, and the chapel is still in use, the Register of Burials will be kept by the minister of the chapel. Where the chapel is closed, the Register of Burials should be in the CRO.

The best known Methodist Burial Grounds are at Wesley's Chapel in London where 5451 burials took place between 1779 and 1854, and at Englesea Brook near Crewe, where Hugh Bourne and other early Primitive Methodists are buried.

6. RECORDS OF AN INDIVIDUAL METHODIST CHAPEL

Methodists have always been very conscientious in keeping written records of chapel meetings and of the many and varied committees within the life of the chapel.

The records of a typical Methodist chapel dating from the early 19th Century may include some of these records.

1. **Baptismal Registers -** [see above].

2. **Marriage Registers** - duplicate copies of marriages from 1898 or from the date when the chapel was registered for marriages – [see above].

3. **Burial Registers -** [see above].

4. **Registers of Members/ Community Roll/ Church Directory -** Many chapels have kept registers of members from the date of opening to the present day or up to the date of closure of a chapel. These registers usually include the address of a member and may include information about the chapel a member had come from or had moved to, as well as recording the death of a member or in some instances "ceased to meet," or "fallen" where a member had stopped attending the chapel.

5. **Class Lists and names of Class Leaders** – These are lists of people who were declared members of the church, who used to meet each week for bible study and prayer at the home of the Class Leader. Members of a chapel are still put in classes but not all classes of today meet on a regular basis as in earlier days. Early 19th century Class Books often give the names of members, their marital status, occupation and address.

6. **Leaders' Meeting Minutes or Church Council Minutes** - These minute books contain the names of chapel members who had been elected to look after the chapel property, and record comments made about the quality of worship in the services and pastoral care of members. The minute books often show the names of all who attended and are sometimes accompanied by an attendance register which everyone present had signed.

7. **Annual Chapel Meeting Minute Books -** These contain annual reports from the different organisations in the chapel and the names of chapel officers elected for the following year. Again these may be accompanied by attendance registers signed by those present.

8. **Society Stewards' Accounts or Chapel Stewards' Accounts** - These show annual income and expenditure of a chapel. Some are summary accounts, but more detailed accounts were often shown in early account books.

9. **Collection Journals and Weekly Offering Ledgers -** These books record details of chapel collections and the names of the ministers and local preachers who took the services.

10. **Pew Rent Records -** Before the Second World War, many chapels were well attended and members paid monthly or quarterly pew rents to reserve their seats.

The rates differed depending on where people sat in the chapel. From these lists it is possible to work out where your ancestors sat – if the pews haven't been replaced by chairs in recent times.

11. **Trustees' Minutes and Memoranda regarding the Appointment of Trustees** - Every chapel was required to appoint trustees who were responsible for the upkeep of the chapel buildings. Trustees were often appointed for life. A new Trust would be formed, every 20-30 years, when half of the old Trust had either died or had moved out of the area.

12. **Sunday School Minutes/ Accounts/ Registers -** Many chapels used to have flourishing Sunday Schools and kept detailed records of scholars' attendances, anniversary services and Sunday School outings.

13. **Choir Minutes -** Often record information about choir members, which parts they sang, special concerts and services in which they participated as well as disputes between choir members and the organist!

14. **Building Fund Minutes and Accounts -** These may include information about chapel extensions, fund raising events and the names of generous donors.

15. **Wesley Guild Minutes/Roll book/Accounts -** Originally a Youth Movement founded in 1896 to retain young people in the Wesleyan Church by holding weekly meetings for devotional, literary and social purposes. By 1909 there were 2,200 local guilds and 152,000 members.

16. **Band of Hope/ Temperance Meeting Minutes/Registers and Accounts** The Band of Hope and Temperance meetings were held to persuade adherents to abstain from drinking anything alcoholic. Those who took the "pledge" were given a certificate and these often turn up in collections of family papers. The Band of Hope Movement was founded in Leeds in1847 to teach children the importance of teetotalism. Many chapels with a Band of Hope Group also had a Band of Hope Choir which took part in circuit and district competitions. The Annual Treat was an important event that often led to entertaining reports in local newspapers and church magazines.

17. **Christian Endeavour Meeting Minutes/Registers and Accounts**.

18. **Youth Club Minutes/Attendance Registers and Accounts**.

19. **Women's Meeting/Ladies' Circle Minutes and Accounts**.

20. **Memorials** – In addition to written records, there are often commemorative wall plaques, and Rolls of Honour/ War Memorials to be found in local chapels. You may also find memorial plaques commemorating men and women who had served as trustees, Sunday School teachers, chapel organists or had been generous benefactors.

There are photographs of hundreds of Methodist War Memorials online on the website Methodist War Memorials. Many of these photographs are accompanied by transcriptions and short biographies. An excellent example is that of Bromley Methodist Church War Memorial which can be found on Google or on www.mymethodisthistory.org.uk Also search "Methodist" on www.ukniwm.org. uk – the UK National Inventory of War Memorials.

7. RECORDS OF A METHODIST CIRCUIT

Every Methodist chapel belongs to a circuit, or belonged to a circuit before the chapel was closed. A circuit may comprise only 2 or 3 chapels in some towns and cities but as many as 20-30 chapels in rural areas. Circuit records may include duplicate records of chapels in the circuit as well as records of the different circuit meetings and organisations.

A typical collection of circuit records may include:

1. **Circuit Registers of Baptisms** – A combined register of baptisms that had taken place in each of the circuit chapels.

2. **Circuit Plans** – List the names and addresses of ministers, local preachers, circuit stewards [who were responsible for the upkeep of all Methodist property in the circuit], as well as showing the preachers' appointments for the three or four month period covered by the plan. The Society of Cirplanologists was formed in 1955 to encourage the study and collection of Methodist circuit plans. It publishes a twice yearly newsletter CIRPLAN. For further information about the Society contact -Mr E A Rose, 26 Roe Cross Green, Mottram, Hyde, Cheshire. SK14 6LP.

3. **Circuit Directories** - Usually published annually showing the names and addresses of all ministers, local preachers, circuit officers and office holders in each chapel in the circuit.

4. **Circuit Quarterly Meeting Minute Books** – Contain summaries of the quarterly business meetings of the circuit and list the names of attendees and those who had given apologies for absence.

5. **Local Preachers' Meeting Minute Books** – Methodism still relies heavily on local preachers [or lay preachers] to conduct services as it has many more chapels than ordained ministers. Local preachers go through a rigorous programme of training before they are "Fully Accredited." The Minute Books record how local preachers progress initially from being "On Note" to being "On Trial" before becoming "Fully Accredited." A considerable number of young local preachers on becoming "Fully Accredited" used to then go forward to train as full-time Methodist ministers and the minute books record the support and encouragement they received from the circuit. There may be a collection of "Preachers' Candidating Forms" attached to the minute books in these cases recording the names of ministers and local preachers who supported the prospective minister's application.

6. **Circuit Property Schedules** - Give information about the condition of each chapel in the circuit. These would have been completed annually by the chapel stewards and received at a Circuit Quarterly Meeting.

7. **Circuit Registers of Members** – Lists of members attending each of the chapels in the circuit. They also record deaths of members, transfers of member-ship between chapels and circuits and sadly some who had ceased to be members.

8. **Circuit Trustees Meeting Minutes** – Contain lists of trustees and minutes of their meetings. Circuits appointed trustees and stewards to be responsible for circuit property, especially the manses in which the ministers lived. Until comparatively recent times the circuit officers were responsible for furnishing the manses as well as maintaining the properties in good condition – some circuits did this as cheaply as possible as the minutes show.

9. **Chapel Registration Certificates** - These confirm that the chapel was a registered place of worship.

10. **Circuit Accounts** - Often include details of expenses incurred when ministers moved to another circuit.

11. **Circuit Class Books** – Lists of the names of members in each chapel and to which classes they were allocated for spiritual and pastoral care.

12. **Circuit Account Books** – May show amounts of money paid to poor members of the circuit out of collections taken "for the Poor Fund" at Communion Services.

13. Many circuits have collections of "**Miscellaneous Records**." These may include items such as reports on the Sunday Schools in the circuit, names of subscribers to the circuit magazine or to a weekly Methodist newspaper, Trip Books listing names of people who went on circuit outings and how much they paid, the Horse Hire Fund or Travel Fund accounts showing expenses paid to ministers and local preachers in the days before bicycles and motor cars.

14. **Chapel Histories** - May record how early Methodists met in private houses before a preaching house or chapel was built. In such cases a "Dissenters' Certificate" or a "Meeting House Certificate" giving permission to meet in a nominated building had to be obtained from a Justice of the Peace and registered in the records of the Quarter Sessions[QS]. A return of all such certificates granted between 1689 -1852 can be found at TNA in Class RG31. Copies of these certificates may be located in chapel, circuit or QS papers and often included the names of some of the members of the founding society.

The Lincolnshire village of Scotter holds the unique distinction of being the only English village to host a National Methodist Conference – the Primitive Methodist Conference of 1829. Methodism had taken root in Scotter by 1771 when a Dissenters' Certificate granted on 14th November 1771 licensed the house of Jonathan Babbins for the use of His Majesty's subjects dissenting from the Church of England commonly called "Independents." The Certificate names the Dissenters as Jonathan Babbins, John Moulson, William Morley, William Wilson, William Shadford, N M Saxton and Richard Lovell.

A subsequent Dissenters' Certificate of June 1774 licences "a house lately built in Scotter" for dissenters called Methodists. Those named were William Morley, Mary Morley, Ann Morley, William Wilson, William Ward, and Grace Ward.

It was quite common for early Methodist meeting houses to be described as "Protestant" or Independent", but they strongly objected to being called Dissenters!

There is an interesting collection of Dissenters' Certificates for the Newbury Circuit in the Berkshire CRO which was found a few years ago during the house clearance of a former circuit steward.

15. **Circuit Magazines** – Similar to Anglican Parish Magazines, these often included articles culled from national and district publications as well as items from the circuit. They are particularly useful for Obituaries and Appreciations.

An excellent example can be found in: **The Keighley Wesleyan Methodist Circuit Magazine – November 1910.**

An Appreciation of **Mr Jesse Mosley**

Mr Jesse Mosley is a worthy example of Methodism of half a century ago. Of his conversion he has not the shadow of doubt. One who knew him at the time says "Mr Mosley was so full of joy at the change that had taken place in him that he could have jumped over the Communion rail."

Jesse Mosley was born at West Lane, Haworth, on the 5th February 1835. Owing to the stress of circumstances in his home he had to commence working full time at the age of nine. He left Haworth when 19 years of age and went to Whitby, and there spent some 14 months preparing timber for clog soles. He then went to Cleveland Dale, near Middlesbrough and after two years' absence from Haworth came to Keighley, a young man of 21 years. He has followed the business of clogger practically the whole of his working days. He is full of happy memories of the work in connection with the Wesleyan Church in the Keighley Circuit and tells the story of the circumstances which led to his conversion with great warmth and depth of feeling. Out of mere curiosity he went to the Temple Street Chapel on Sunday morning in 1867 and found himself somewhat late for the service which commenced at that date at 10 o'clock. The late Mr William Stead, who was chapel keeper, showed him into a pew in the middle of the chapel. Curiosity had led him to the house of worship to hear the Rev John Rhodes who was known as the "Weeping Prophet" preach. He found that the preacher he had expected to see and hear was not in the pulpit, the service being conducted by Rev John Raynor who was then Supernumerary. He remembers the subject quite well, it being Mary and Martha. It was the last sermon preached by Mr Raynor in the Temple Street Chapel and to Mr Mosley it was the first sermon heard in that chapel and was the starting point of better days. He went again and heard the Rev Peter Featherstone preach and was brought under deep conviction. He says, "I did not get brought in," but Mr John Smith, joiner, of Green Street, who was then one of the principal workers of Temple Street, came and spoke to him kindly about matters referring to his spiritual welfare. He stayed to the prayer meeting but still did not receive release from his anxieties. He came again on the Thursday evening. "It was a great day for me was that day." Mr Joshua Normington was preaching about Paul and Silas. It was at this service that he was set free. It was the commencement of better days, and he says he has never lost his confidence since. He was soon harnessed to work by the Temple Street friends, and for 30 years he was one of the Sunday School Visitors, having for his companions at different times Mr John Stell, Mr Alfred Lord, Mr Edward Sharp, and Mr Robert Clough [Highfield Lane]. He was appointed to lead the Class of the late Mr John Pickles, father of Mr David Pickles and Mr H Pickles and is still the leader of this Class. He says that he has seen many revivals, but the revival in his own life in 1867 was the greatest of them all. He has pleasant recollections of many of the prominent workers of the past: the Rev Michael Johnson, the Rev John Brash, Mr Edmund Laycock, Mr Johnson Hugill, Mr Benjamin Butterfield, Mr Richard Newton, Mr Thomas Butterfield, Mr Thomas Rhodes, Mr Richard Mitchell, Miss Mary Wright and Miss Martha Wright.

He deplores not having had the privileges of a day school education, and refers to some of the troubles and grave anxieties which he has passed through, and is thankful for the hand which has been with him and assisted him through them all. Mrs Mosley died some 12 years ago. Mr Mosley is of a bright, genial disposition and his testimony in Fellowship Meetings, Love Feasts and Prayer Meetings are always appreciated and many of the younger members have been encouraged to new and better lives as a result of the cheerful and encouraging words spoken by him. The members of the Church with which he has been so long connected heartily pray that Mr Mosley may have continued brightness and comfort to the end of the days that are granted to him.

Wm Robertshaw.

8. OTHER USEFUL SOURCES

Local Newspapers

Local Newspapers are a rich source of information about Methodist activities in local chapels or of circuit events. There may be reports about Sunday services and weekday meetings, Chapel Anniversaries, Sunday School Anniversaries, Chapel and Sunday School Outings, Boys' Brigade and Girls' Brigade activities, Choir Concerts, Circuit Rallies – especially the annual celebration of Wesley Day on May 24th, and pen portraits of prominent local worthies some of whom were Methodists. For a comprehensive index of holdings of Local Newspapers see *Local Newspapers 1750-1920 in England Wales, Channel Islands and IOM – a select location list* [third edition] Jeremy Gibson, Family History Partnership [2011].

Many newspapers can now be consulted online with many public libraries offering free access to the 19th Century British newspapers database. Subscription websites include the British Library Archive on www.britishlibraryarchive.co.uk . See also British Newspapers 1710-1965 at www.findmypast.co.uk

Census Returns

Census returns between 1851 and 1911 are another source for locating Methodist ancestry. They record a minister's occupation as "Wesleyan Methodist Minister" or

"Primitive Methodist Minister" and some local preachers are recorded as "Farmer and Wesleyan Methodist Local Preacher." In some instances children are recorded as "Methodist Sunday School scholars."

In 1851 as well as the National Census, a voluntary **Ecclesiastical Census** of worshippers was taken. The complete set of records of this Census is held at The National Archives and is arranged by County or by Poor Law Union. CROs and Local Studies Libraries may hold copies of the Ecclesiastical Census, originally published in the Parliamentary Papers series for their local areas. Ecclesiastical Census returns have recently been re- published for some counties.

When compiled by the Home Office, the Ecclesiastical Census gave details of the location of every place of worship in England and Wales and the total attendances at all services and Sunday Schools held on Census Sunday, 30th March 1851. The Ecclesiastical Census also gives the average attendances for each place of worship for the previous 12 months.

E.g., the Ecclesiastical Return for the Wesleyan Preaching Room at Badsey, near Evesham in Worcestershire shows that the Preaching Room was part of a dwelling house with seating for 60 people. On Census Sunday, the morning congregation was 40 and the evening congregation was 42. These figures compared with average morning congregations for the previous 12 months of 35, and 45 in the evening services. No figures are recorded of Sunday School scholars. The return was signed by Robert Taylor, Society Steward at Badsey.

The Ecclesiastical Census of Scotter [Lincolnshire] shows that there were 3 Methodist chapels in a village with a population of 1158. Attendances on the 30th March, 1851 were – Wesleyan Chapel – morning 68, evening 73; Primitive Chapel – morning 200, evening 300; Methodist New Connexion Chapel – morning 112, evening 156. If these figures are accurate 67% of the population of Scotter in 1851 were Methodists!

Diaries and Journals

Many early Methodists kept diaries not dissimilar to Wesley's Journal. These may be found in CROs or Local Studies Libraries, either in manuscript form or in published limited editions. They make interesting reading as they mention chapels, class meetings and services that the diary writers attended and the names of people whom they met or stayed with on their travels. An excellent example is *"Journals of a Methodist Farmer 1871-1875",* ed. Jean Stovin, Croom Helm Ltd, 1982, which are the journals of Cornelius Stovin, tenant farmer of Binbrook, Lincolnshire, and a founder member of Binbrook Free Methodist Chapel.

9. METHODIST HERITAGE and ARCHIVES

In 2008 the Methodist Conference received a report highlighting the untapped potential of the Methodist Church's historic sites and archives. The Conference responded by setting up a Methodist Heritage Committee "to conserve and make accessible to visitors Methodist artefacts, archives, historic sites, and listed chapels."

It appointed a full-time Heritage Officer to co-ordinate and support its heritage resources. The Committee plans to publish every two years a comprehensive Visitors' Guide to Methodist Heritage Sites and Archives. The Guide is available FREE of charge - for details of how to obtain a copy see www.Methodistheritage.org.uk. Researchers can also sign up to a twice yearly Methodist Heritage Newsletter.

Several new Methodist websites have recently been created - My Methodist History www.mymethodisthistory.org.uk ; My Primitive Methodist Ancestors www. MyPrimitiveMethodists.org.uk; My Wesleyan Methodist Ancestors www.My WesleyanMethodists.org.uk. Additionally the site www.mymethodisthistory.org.uk allows the exchange of information related to Methodist history.

The Methodist Heritage Visitors' Guide lists several Methodist Archives. The principal Methodist Archives are listed below.

Methodist Archives and Research Centre [MARC]

The largest collections of Methodist Connexional Records have been deposited at the **John Rylands University Library, 150 Deansgate, Manchester M3 3EH** www.library.manchester.ac.uk/deansgate

The Methodist Conference of 1961 set up the **Methodist Archives and Research Centre** [MARC]. This was originally located at Wesley's Chapel in City Road, London, but was transferred to Manchester in 1977.

MARC hold the records of the Annual Conference, the District Synods, those of the National Officers and the Divisions [or Departments] of the Methodist Church, but generally it does not hold chapel and circuit records.

MARC holds over 60,000 printed records and several hundred thousand manuscripts, relating to all the branches of Methodism that existed before Methodist Union in 1932 as well as the world's largest collection of manuscripts relating to John and Charles Wesley.

MARC also holds substantial collections of manuscripts relating to other early Methodists such as John Fletcher of Madeley, Thomas Coke, William Clowes, Hugh Bourne, Joseph Benson and Jabez Bunting and prominent evangelical contemporaries of the Wesleys such as George Whitfield, Selina, Countess of Huntingdon, Howel Harris and Benjamin Ingham.

There are considerable collections of records of all the major pre-union Methodist denominations including the Lewis Court Bible Christian Collection.

The connexional records are of most help to researchers carrying out in depth research on Methodism and to family and local historians who are interested in the history of a particular chapel or circuit. There are good collections of Methodist chapel histories and Methodist newspapers and journals which contain much biographical information about ministers, local preachers and prominent Methodist laymen. Other connexional records include the world's largest collection of preaching plans, Methodist education records, the archives of three Methodist ministerial training colleges, [Handsworth, Hartley Victoria and Richmond], the Armed Forces Board collection of Methodist Chaplains in Britain and many overseas countries and the archives of the Methodist Districts, especially Wesleyan, after 1791.

MARC also has complete sets of the Minutes of Conference of all the branches of Methodism.

Researchers are welcome to use the library facilities at the John Rylands University Library[JRL] which is a 20 minute walk from Manchester Piccadilly Rail Station, but are advised to contact Dr Peter Nockles, Assistant Librarian [Methodist Collections] [0161 275 3755] or e-mail peter.nockles@man.ac.uk before making a visit. A letter of recommendation and some form of identity is required for the first visit so that a JRL Readers' ticket can be issued. There are several online catalogues available to help plan a visit to the Library on ELGAR, see http://archives.li.man.ac.uk/ead

Wesley and Methodist Studies Centre

The **Wesley and Methodist Studies Centre,** based at Oxford Brookes University, houses the second most important printed collection relating to British Methodism. The Centre has a good collection of local histories, chapel histories, Methodist newspapers and journals as well as copies of Hill's Arrangements 1819-1968, Hall's Circuits 1765-1925, Leary's Circuits 1924-1980 [in typescript] and Methodist Who's Who 1910-15 and 1933.[See selected bibliography]

The Centre also holds complete sets of Minutes of Conference, Conference Brochures, Agendas and accompanying Conference papers and reports. It also holds extensive collections of bound copies of various Methodist Magazines from 1770 onwards, as well as bound and microfilmed copies of the Methodist Recorder [1861-2005], The Watchman [1835-1884], and bound volumes of the Wesleyan Sunday School Magazine which contain Sunday School lessons and obituaries of Sunday School teachers.

It also houses the Archives of Westminster College which used to be a male teacher training college in Horseferry Road, Westminster. These Archives include Annual Reports of the Wesleyan Methodist Education Committee, obituaries of Wesleyan teachers; testimonials of Wesleyan teachers, a card index of deceased Westminster-ians and a register of students who completed their training and to which schools they were appointed.

Researchers are welcome but prior booking is advised via Dr Peter Forsaith, Methodist Heritage Co-ordinator, Methodist Studies Unit, Westminster Institute of Education, Oxford Brookes University, Harcourt Hill, Oxford. OX2 9AT [Tel: 01865 488319] or e-mail pforsaith@brookes.ac.uk or wco.archives@brookes.ca.uk .

Wesley's Chapel

Wesley's Chapel in City Road, London contains the Museum of Methodism in the crypt where many artefacts associated with John Wesley and early Methodist leaders can be seen. Opened in 1984 it is currently being refurbished. Phase 1 was completed in 2013 and Phase 2 when funds permit.

Next door is Wesley's House built at the same time as the Chapel in 1779. It was here that John Wesley slept when in London and also where he died on March 2nd, 1791. Behind Wesley's Chapel is a Methodist Burial ground where John Wesley was buried on March 9th at 5.00 a.m. 5450 other burials took place here between 1779 and 1854. These have been transcribed and indexed by the London and North Middlesex Family History Society and are available for purchase as a set of microfiche from the Society. Opposite Wesley's Chapel is Bunhill Fields, a large Nonconformist burial ground containing the grave of Susannah Wesley, John Wesley's mother.

For further information contact the Administrator- administration@wesleys chapel.org.uk or by phoning 020 7253 2262 or visit the website:www.wesleyschapel. org.uk

Englesea Brook Chapel and Museum

Englesea Brook Chapel and Museum, near Crewe, Cheshire, CW2 5QW is the location of the **Museum of Primitive Methodism**. It houses over 3000 PM artefacts including a large collection of PM Circuit plans listing ministers, local preachers and chapel officers, a Library of PM literature which includes bound copies of PM Magazines containing reports of chapel openings and obituaries of men, women and children, and a complete set of PM Minutes of Conferences from 1819-1932.

The Library is open to researchers by appointment via the Project Director engleseabrook-methodist-museum@supanet.com .

The Museum holds regular series of talks, open days, etc, details of which can be found on www.myprimitivemethodists.org.uk or by phoning 01270 820836.

Details of opening times can be found at www.methodistheritage.org.uk/englesea brook.htm

The New Room

The New Room [John Wesley's Chapel], 36 The Horsefair, Bristol. BS1 3JE - John Wesley's Chapel in Bristol is the oldest Methodist chapel in the world. Built in 1739 it is open throughout the year on Mondays- Saturdays from 10.00am-4.00pm each day. Further information can be obtained by telephoning 0117 926 4740. It houses an extensive library of over 3,500 volumes of Methodist history. Online information on www.newroombristol.org.uk or Email: info@newroombristol.org.uk.

The National Archives

The National Archives at Kew holds a microfilm copy of the Wesleyan Methodist Metropolitan Registry which contains 10341 baptismal certificates which were registered at the Wesleyan Methodist Register Office, 66 Paternoster Row, near St Paul's Church, London between 1818 and 1838. There is an index - RG4/4680 and the certificates can be located in RG4/4677, 4678 and 4679. This is in addition to the 856 volumes of Methodist Baptism and Burials Registers which were surrendered to the Registrar General in 1837. All of these registers can be searched online at www.bmdregisters,co.uk.

The British Library Newspaper Library
The British Library Newspaper Library has extensive collections of Methodist newspapers including The Watchman [1835-1884], The Methodist Times, [1885-1932] The Primitive Methodist [1868-1932] and The Methodist Recorder [1861 to date], The Primitive Methodist Leader 1905-1925], The Methodist Leader [1926-1932], The Methodist Times and Leader [1932-1937] and The Primitive Methodist World and Sunday School Worker [1883-1908]. Copies of articles, etc., in the Methodist Recorder from 1861 can be obtained from the Methodist Studies Unit, Oxford Brookes University – see above.

Westminster Methodist Central Hall
Westminster Methodist Central Hall Archives and Visitor Centre, Storey's Gate, London SW1H 9NH contains the unique **Wesleyan Methodist Historic Roll**. This is a good starting off point to see if any of your ancestors may have been Wesleyan Methodists c.1900 and links in very well to the 1901 Census. The 50 volumes contain the names and addresses of over one million donors in 815 Circuits in England, Scotland, Wales and Overseas who contributed to the Wesleyan Methodist Twentieth Century [or Million Guinea] Fund between 1899 and 1904. The whereabouts of the volume containing over 50,000 donors in Ireland is not known. For detailed information about this important archive see *Basic Facts about The Wesleyan Methodist Historic Roll, Richard Ratcliffe, [FFHS] 2005* which is available from the Visitors' Centre at Westminster Methodist Central Hall visitorservices@ c-h-w.org.uk or on 020 7654 3826. Some Family History Societies and The Eureka Partnership www.eurekapartnership.com have published transcriptions of the Historic Roll for their local area.
Among much interesting information to be gleaned from the Historic Roll are the names of family members of donors who had emigrated and were living overseas at the time. An example is this list of emigrants in Volume 13 - The Cornwall District

Redruth Circuit
P6 Mrs Lily WILLIAMS and Mr H Arthur WILLIAMS – Pietermaritzburg, S Africa
P8 Fdk John RICH, Josephine RICH, Howard Fdk RICH – Mount Donaldson Mine, Corinna, Tasmania
P9 John JAMES, Emily E JAMES, Emily Elizabeth JAMES, Susan E JAMES, Mabel A B JAMES, Lillie JAMES – 3748 N Carlisle St, Philadelphia.

Camborne Circuit
P22 Wm BOND, Jnr, Ada BOND + 3 children – Rio Tinto, Spain
P25 John Edgar RABLING, Henry Lambert RABLING – Pachuca, Mexico
P31 Hugh Severin STEPHENS – Walcha, N S W
P33 Thomas Martin LOWRY – Mount Leonora, W Australia
P33 Hubert Edmund JEFFERY – Holai Gold Fields, India
P48 T H OXNAM, Mamie OXNAM – 1026 Wall St, Los Angeles, California

Falmouth Circuit
P68 Lilian BARLEY [nee DEWSTOE] – Barrackpore, Calcutta
P68 Nellie Gertrude NICHOLLS [nee DEWSTOE] Tocopilla, Chile

Truro Circuit
P101 Dorothy Lester NORTHCROFT – Mission House, Abaco, Bahamas

St Austell Circuit
P214 Francis Stocker KING and Herbert Jeffrey KING – Laramie, Wyoming, USA.

St Mawes Circuit
P238 Mary Ellen PHILLIPS – Richardson County, Nebraska, USA

Penzance Circuit
P307 Julia LADNER [late Penzance] now Philadelphia
P339 Joseph Wallis JAMES – Capetown, S Africa
P339 John MADDERN – Woodville, S Australia

Helston Circuit
P437 Lilian M DOWER and Leelia J DOWER – Westerley, Rhode Island, USA

Hayle Circuit
P511 Gilbert PEARCE Jnr – Singapore
P511 Richard Donald PEARCE and Mary V PEARCE – Johannesburg

Marazion Circuit
P543 Ellen Mabel MITCHELL – Tokai, Cape Colony, S Africa

Wesley Centre, Wednesbury
Wesley Centre, Wednesbury Central Methodist Church, Spring Head, Wednesbury, West Midlands. WS10 9AD holds a collection of Archives collected by Dr Dingley and artefacts connected to the Wednesbury Riots of 1743-44. Further information – contact the Centre Manager centre.manager@wesleycentre forall.com or on 0121 556 0420.

School of Oriental and African Studies [SOAS**]**
School of Oriental and African Studies Library, University of London, Thornhaugh Street, Russell Square, London WC1H OXG. SOAS holds the Archives of the Methodist Missionary Society and the Methodist Missionary Society Library. Readers require a relevant ticket and for the first visit need to bring a letter of recommendation from the Methodist Church, e.g. a minister or church officer. Further information contact the Archivist docenquiry@soas.ac.uk or on 020 7898 4180.

10. METHODIST RECORDS IN SCOTLAND

The **National Archives in Scotland** holds an extensive collection of records of Wesleyan and Primitive Methodist Circuits and District Synods in Scotland in Class CH11 from 1764 onwards.

The principal records held are Circuit Minute Books, Baptismal Registers, Membership Lists, Pew [Seat] rents, Sunday School attendance registers, correspondence and bundles of miscellaneous records such as circuit plans, orders of services and published accounts. It should be noted that all Scottish Methodist Church records are closed for 30 years from the date of the last entry in that record.

Records of a confidential nature are closed for 75 years from the date of the last entry, unless permission has been granted to an individual in writing from the relevant church or circuit. Confidential records include disciplinary matters involving ministers or church members, complaints, statements of ministers and pastoral matters. A full list of deposited Methodist records can be found on the National Archives of Scotland website <www.nas.gov.uk>.

11. METHODIST RECORDS IN WALES

A large number of early Welsh Methodist Birth/Baptismal and Burial Registers up to 1837 were surrendered to the Registrar General in 1840 and are held by The National Archives. Microfilmed copies of these registers can be seen at the **National Library of Wales**, Penglais Road, Aberystwyth, SA23 3BU, at CROs in Wales and at Family History Centres of the Church of the Latter Day Saints. Registers surrendered in 1840 included those of a large number of Welsh Calvinist Methodist Chapels which by then had become part of the Presbyterian Church of Wales, a small number of Welsh Wesleyan Chapels and Welsh Calvinist Chapels in the predominantly Welsh speaking counties of Cardiganshire and Merionethshire. The full list can be found in William Leary's "My Ancestors were Methodists" 4th edition [SOG] 2006.

Deposited Welsh Methodist records after 1837 can be located in the National Library of Wales and in CROs in Wales. A useful chapter on Welsh Nonconformity by Muriel Bowen Evans can be found in *"Welsh Family History: A Guide to Research"* edited by John & Sheila Rowlands [Second edition] 1998.

It is worth noting that there were a number of Welsh speaking Wesleyan Methodist Circuits outside Wales in London, Liverpool, Manchester, Hanley, Leeds and Stockton on Tees that existed well into the 20th Century.

Contact details for the National Library of Wales are: <llgc.org.uk> or on 01970 632800.

12. METHODIST RECORDS IN IRELAND

Tracing Methodist ancestors in Ireland is far from easy! Although there have been Methodists in Ireland since the 1740s, the Irish Methodist Conference only voted to allow the Sacraments of Baptism and Holy Communion in their preaching houses or chapels in 1818. Methodist chapels were not licensed for marriages before 1863 although marriages took place in Methodist chapels from 1845 provided the District Registrar was in attendance.

While the Irish Methodist Connexion was the largest Methodist denomination in Ireland, four smaller branches existed in Ireland for much of the 19th Century. The Primitive Wesleyan Methodists [PWM] were a group of about 8,000 members who broke away from the Irish Methodists after 1818 as they wished to remain loyal to the Church of Ireland. Their baptisms and marriages continued to take place in the parish church with no indication in the registers of their Methodist links. The PWMs published a magazine between 1823-1878 which reported on chapel openings and included obituaries. The PWMs reunited with the main Methodist Connexion in 1878.

The three other smaller branches were The Methodist New Connexion [1789-1905], the Primitive Methodist Connexion [1823-1910] and the Wesleyan Methodist Association [1832-1872].

The vast majority of Methodist Baptismal and Marriage Registers are still held by local Methodist chaples and may be consulted via the minister of the chapel. The largest collection of deposited registers and other Methodist archives is held by the **Methodist Historical Society of Ireland** [MHSI] at Edgehill College, Belfast. The **Dublin District** has a large collection of registers at Christ Church, Sandy Mount, Dublin.

Initial enquiries regarding Irish Methodist records should be made via the Archivist, MSHI, Edgehill College, Belfast. Please note that the Society does not provide a genealogical research service.

See also <www.irishmethodist.org/genealogy-services>

13. METHODIST SCHOOLS and COLLEGES of HIGHER EDUCATION

John Wesley founded the first Methodist School at Kingswood in Bristol in 1748. It later moved to Bath in 1852 and was principally a boarding school offering a stable education to children of Methodist ministers who were constantly moving circuits every two or three years. Today there are 14 Independent Methodist Schools in England and Wales and 2 Methodist Colleges in Ireland. Many began like Kingswood as boarding schools for children of Methodist ministers and most have substantial archives.

The Wesley Centre at Kingswood School, Lansdown Road, Bath, Somerset. BA1 5RG holds an extensive amount of information of interest to family and Wesleyan historians in its archives. For more information contact the School Archivist on 01255 734352 or by e-mail <wesleycentre@kingswood.bath.sch.uk>.

For a list of the other Methodist Independent Schools and Colleges such as the former Southlands Teacher Training College, now part of Brunel University, see <www.methodisteducation.co.uk>

There are also 57 Methodist or joint Anglican/Methodist Primary Schools in England and Wales, many of which were founded with the help of the British and Foreign Schools Society [BFSS] after 1814. The BFSS archive is now located at the Old School House, 1 Hillingdon Hill, Uxbridge, Middlesex UB10 0AA, close to Brunel University's Uxbridge Campus. For more information contact bfss.archive@brunel. ac.uk or on 01895 267095.

14. IMPORTANT PRINTED SOURCES

There are a number of printed books that may be of use to family historians seeking information about Methodist ancestors. These include:

Hills' Arrangements - Lists of ministers and their stations originally compiled by Rev William Hill in 1819 and published thereafter every 3-4 years until 1988.

An example from the 1947 edition edited by Rev J Henry Martin, Methodist Publishing House.

Workman, Herbert B, MA, D.Litt., DD. [Wesleyan] – Didsbury
1885 Didsbury College, Assistant Tutor
1888 Birmingham, Moseley Road
1891 Bristol, Redland
1894 Liverpool, Brunswick
1897 Newcastle, Brunswick
1898 Birmingham, Moseley Road
1901 Aberdeen
1903 Westminster Training College, Principal
1930 Secretary, Methodist Education Dept
1940 Supernumerary
President of the Wesleyan Conference, 1930.

Garlick's Methodist Registry, 1983 – Kenneth B Garlick, Edsall of London, 1983 – Brief biographies of Methodist ministers compiled from information supplied by ministers, with some useful appendices.
A good example is:

Soper, Donald Oliver, Hinde Street Methodist Church, W1.
MA [Cantab], PhD [London]. Born 31 Jan 1903, Wandsworth, Married 3 Aug 1927 – 4 daughters.
Education - 1915-20 Askes Haberdashers; 1921-24 Cambridge Univ; 1924-26 Wesley House.

Appointments – 1926-29 S London Mission; London Mission: 1936-78 West London Mission.
Parliamentary Service – 1963- Peerage.
Connexional Committees – 1953 President of the Conference.
Local Council Committees – 1960-63 LCC.
Hobbies and Recreations; Games, Music.

Hall's Circuits and Ministers in Great Britain from 1765-1925 - Compiled by Rev Joseph Hall in 1925, since updated to 1980 by Rev William Leary.

Directory of Primitive Methodist Ministers and their Circuits - Rev William Leary, Teamprint, Loughborough, [1990].Lists ministers and their circuits from 1819-1932.

The United Methodist Church, Ministers and their Circuits - Dr Oliver A Beckerlegge [1968] - Lists ministers in the branches of Methodism which came together to form the United Methodist Church in 1907, i.e. the Methodist New Connexion, the Bible Christians, the Wesleyan Association and the United Methodist Free Churches.

The Story of the United Methodist Church – ed. Henry Smith, John E Swallow and William Treffry, Henry Hooks [1932] includes lists of ministers and their circuits from 1797-1932.

Who's Who in Methodism, published annually between 1910 and 1915 and in 1933 immediately after Methodist Union. It gives brief biographical details of ministers and laymen at the time of publication.

An example from Methodist Who's Who [1914]:

Curnock, Rev Nehemiah – *b. March 30, 1840, son of Rev Nehemiah Curnock, married Sarah Baron Corderoy of Clapham Park, London, 2 sons and 5 daughters.*

Educated at Woodhouse Grove and Didsbury College. Entered [Wesleyan] ministry 1860, Army Chaplain and Circuit Minister until 1886. Editor of Methodist Recorder until 1908. Hon. Librarian, Allan Library; Secretary of Methodist Hymn and Song Book Committee, Peoples' Hymnary and the Methodist School Hymnal and Tune Book Committees.

Publications: Nature Musings, History of the Children's Home [later known as the National Children's Homes], Memorable Nights of the Bible; Editor of Standard Edition of Wesley's Journal.

Recreations: Natural Science and photography.

Address[in 1910] 16 Old Road West, Gravesend.

The Methodist Preacher's Who's Who, 1934 – is similar in format to Who's Who in Methodism and gives brief biographical details of over 25,000 Methodist Local Preachers living at the time of publication.

An example from this publication:

> **Tams, John**, *Born 1880 Staffordshire. Educated at West Hill, Hednesford, married Lottie Boyden, 2 sons and 2 daughters. Supt of Boys' Home. Year admitted as Local Preacher 1903 in Leeds Cardigan St Circuit. Circuit Offices held: Circuit Local Preachers Secretary, member of Local Preachers Examination Committee, Ex-President of Christian Endeavour, Sunday School Treasurer, Circuit Meeting Secretary.*
>
> *Publications – Composer of Hymns and Tunes.*
>
> *Recreations; painting, football, cricket, tennis.*
>
> *Occupations - Successively Iron Moulder, Insurance Agent, Commercial Traveller, Business on own account, Supt of Boys' Home since 1924.*
>
> *Address [in 1934] Boys' Home, 127b Brudenell Rd, Leeds 6.*

Dictionary of Methodism of Britain and Ireland which was published in 2000 is now searchable online at:

> www.wesleyhistoricalsociety.org.uk/dmbi. It contains over 3,500 entries at present and is regularly being updated.

All the above books can be found in the principal Methodist archives previously mentioned and some may also be found in CRO Libraries and Local Studies Libraries.

15. METHODIST HISTORY – a Select Bibliography

Leary, William, *My Ancestor was a Methodist* 4th edition, SOG [2006].

Milburn, Geoffrey, *Primitive Methodism,* Epworth Press [2002].

Tabraham, Barrie W., *The Making of Methodism* [Second edition, revised and updated] , Epworth Press [2010].

Tabraham, Barrie W., *Brother Charles*, Epworth Press [2003].

Turner, John Munsey, *Wesleyan Methodism,* Epworth Press [2005].

Turner, John Munsey *Modern Methodism in England 1932-1998* Epworth Press [1998] .

Wakefield, Gordon S., *John Wesley,* Foundery Press [1990].

Wakefield, Gordon S., *Methodist Spirituality,* Epworth Press [1999].

Hattersley, Roy, *John Wesley, a Brand from the Burning*, Abacus [2002].

Greetham, Mary & Peter, *Samuel Wesley of Epworth*, Foundery Press [1990].

Vickers, John A., *Charles Wesley,* Foundery Press [1990].

Greetham, Mary *Susanna Wesley Mother of Methodism,* Foundery Press [1994].

Maser, Frederick E., *The Wesley Sisters,* Foundery Press [1990].

Parker, Percy Livingstone, *John Wesley's Journal*, Hodder & Stoughton [1993].

Davey, Cyril, *Mad about Mission – The story of Thomas Coke,* Marshalls [1985].

Waddy, J. Leonard., *The Bitter Sacred Cup – The Wednesbury Riots 1743-44,* Pinhorns [1976].

Dallimore, Arnold A., *Susanna,* Evangelical Press [1992].

Curran, David, *Methodism in South Holland, Lincolnshire,* Privately published [2012].

Brooks, Alan, *West End Methodism: the story of Hinde Street,* Northway Publications [2010].

Bourne, F. W., *The Bible Christians: their origins and history 1815-1900,* 2nd edition, Tentmaker Publications [2004].

Batty, Margaret, *Scottish Methodists 1750-2000* Birlinn [2010].

Leetooze, Sherrell Branton, *The Damascus Road: the Bible Christian preachers of the Canadian Conference 1832-1884* Lynn Michael-John Associates [2005].

Shaw, Thomas, *The Bible Christians 1815-1907,* Epworth Press [1965].

Wickes, Michael, *The West-country Preachers; a history of the Bible Christians 1815-1907,* Michael Wickes [1987].

16. A METHODIST CALENDAR

1703 Jun 17	Birth of John Wesley at Epworth in Lincolnshire.
1707 Dec 18	Birth of Charles Wesley at Epworth in Lincolnshire.
1725 Sep 25	John Wesley ordained Deacon in Anglican Church.
1726 Mar 17	John Wesley elected Fellow of Lincoln College, Oxford.
1729	Methodist Society formed at Oxford University.
1735 Oct	John Wesley sailed for Georgia.
1738 Feb 1	John Wesley lands at Deal after turbulent time in Georgia.
1738 May 24	John Wesley's Aldersgate Street conversion.
1739 Apr 2	John Wesley's first open air sermon in Bristol.
1739 Jun 5	New Room, Bristol opened for public worship.
1739	First schoolhouse built at Kingswood, Bristol.
1739	Foundery Chapel in Moorfields, London opened.
1742 Jul	Death of Susanna Wesley "The mother of Methodism." She was buried in Bunhill Fields Nonconformist Burial Ground.
1743-44	The Wednesbury Riots.
1744 Jun 25	First Methodist Conference held in the Foundery Chapel.
1748 Jun 24	John Wesley opened enlarged Kingswood School, Bristol.
1760s	First overseas Methodists in Antigua and America.
1769	First Methodist preachers volunteer to go to America.
1778 Jan	John Wesley launched Arminian Magazine.
1778 Nov	Opening of Wesley's Chapel in City Road, London.
1780	John Wesley published his hymnbook "A Collection of Hymns for the Use of the People called Methodists."

1784 Sep 2	John Wesley ordained Coke, Whatcoat and Vasey as missionaries to the United States of America.
1786	First missionaries sent to the West Indies.
1788 Mar 29	Death of Charles Wesley.
1790 Oct 6	John Wesley's last open air sermon at Winchelsea.
1791 Feb 23	John Wesley's last sermon at Leatherhead.
1791 Mar 2	Death of John Wesley.
1797	Methodist New Connexion founded.
1807	Primitive Methodist Connexion founded.
1814	First missionaries sent to Asia.
1815	Bible Christians founded.
1815	First missionaries sent to Australia.
1818	Wesleyan Missionary Society founded.
1827	Protestant Methodist Connexion founded.
1834	Beginning of Ministerial training.
1834	Wesleyan Methodist Association founded.
1834	Tolpuddle Martyrs.
1849	Wesleyan Reform Movement founded.
1857	United Methodist Free Church Connexion formed.
1899 Jan 1	Wesleyan Methodist Twentieth Century Fund launched – Historic Roll opened.
1904 Jun 30	Wesleyan Methodist Twentieth Century Fund closed having raised £1,073,682.
1907	United Methodist Church formed.
1908	Historic Roll collated into 50 volumes.
1912 Oct 3	Westminster Methodist Central Hall opened – Historic Roll put on public display.
1932 Oct	Methodist Church formed by unification of United Methodist, Primitive Methodist and Wesleyan Methodist Churches. Rev J. Scott Lidgett and Sir Robert W Perks – President and Vice President of the Uniting Conference held in Royal Albert Hall.
1933	Methodist Hymn Book published, as was "Methodist Who's Who" to celebrate Methodist Union.
1946 Jan/Feb	Inaugural session of United Nations Assembly held in Westminster Methodist Central Hall [Great Hall].
1983	Methodist Hymn Book replaced by Hymns and Psalms in many Methodist Churches.
2003	Bicentenary of Birth of John Wesley celebrated in Lincoln Cathedral.
2003 Nov	Anglican-Methodist Covenant signed by H. M. Queen Elizabeth II in Westminster Methodist Central Hall.
2011	New Methodist Hymnbook "Singing the Faith" published.

17. ACKNOWLEDGEMENTS

This book is an updated and revised edition of my earlier book *"Basic Facts about Methodist Records for Family Historians"* published by FFHS Publications [2005] and now out of print.

The most important change since then has been the decision of the Methodist Conference of 2008 to set up a Methodist Heritage Committee and appoint a full-time Methodist Heritage Officer, Jo Hibbard, who is based at Methodist Church House, 25 Marylebone Road, London NW1 5JR hibbardj@methodistchurch.org.uk. Jo is the editor of the extremely popular Visitors' Guide to Methodist Heritage Sites and Archives giving information about 120 Methodist heritage sites and 9 archives and museums and of the half yearly 8 page full colour booklet "Heritage News." To obtain FREE copies of these books visit www.Methodistheritage.org.uk or resources@methodistchurch.org.uk or call 01733 235962.

I hope you find the information contained in this book helpful in finding out more about your known and as yet unknown Methodist ancestors. I am grateful for the help of Dr Peter Forsaith, Dr Janet Few, Stuart Raymond and Stephen Maddrell in preparing this new edition. Please consider reporting your successes on the new Methodist Heritage websites mentioned earlier – you might discover even more Methodist connections by so doing. Happy hunting!

Richard Ratcliffe
Warwick
January, 2014